PRESENTED BY **UNIQVISE** INSIGHTFUL BOOKS

FOR BUSINESS ENQUIRIES EMAIL AT: "UNIQVISE@GMAIL.COM"

Atoms are made up of even tiny pieces called particles. There are 3 main types:

> Say hi to each type that I gave below!

protons and neutrons in the middle (called the nucleus) ; electrons that zoom around the outside.

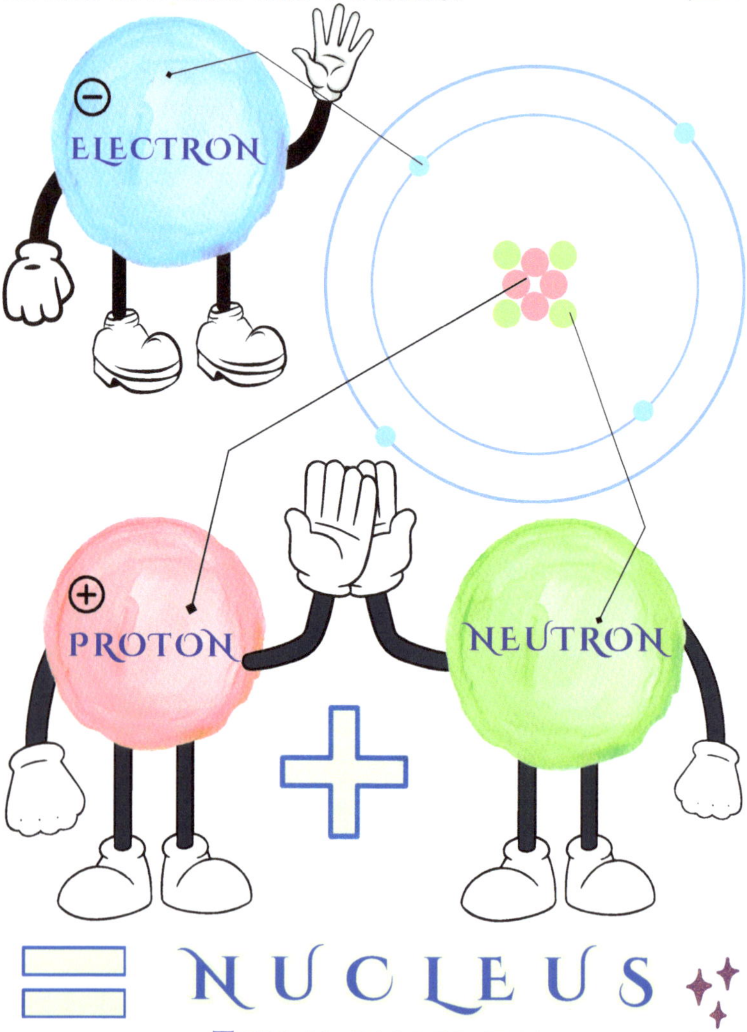

ELECTRON

PROTON   NEUTRON

➕

═ NUCLEUS

THIS IS CALLED TEAM WORK!

Light, like the sunshine and the light from lamps, can behave like both a wave and a particle.

That means it can travel in waves or as tiny bits of energy called photons!

"Isn't light amazing", said Riley. "It can act like both a wave in the ocean and a tiny particle. Let's slide to see how it changes!"

PARENT NOTE

Wave-Particle Duality: Light can behave like both waves and particles, depending on how we look at it!

In the tiny world of quantum physics, things can be in more than one place at the same time! This is called superposition. Superposition means that tiny particles, like the ones that make up everything around us, can exist in multiple states at once until we look at them.

Throw a dice! It will be showing different numbers.

I show you two side of mine, four and five, it's on you to choose side to see.

Hi, Rily here again. Imagine, In the quantum world, things can be in two different places or states at once. It's like having two options at once!

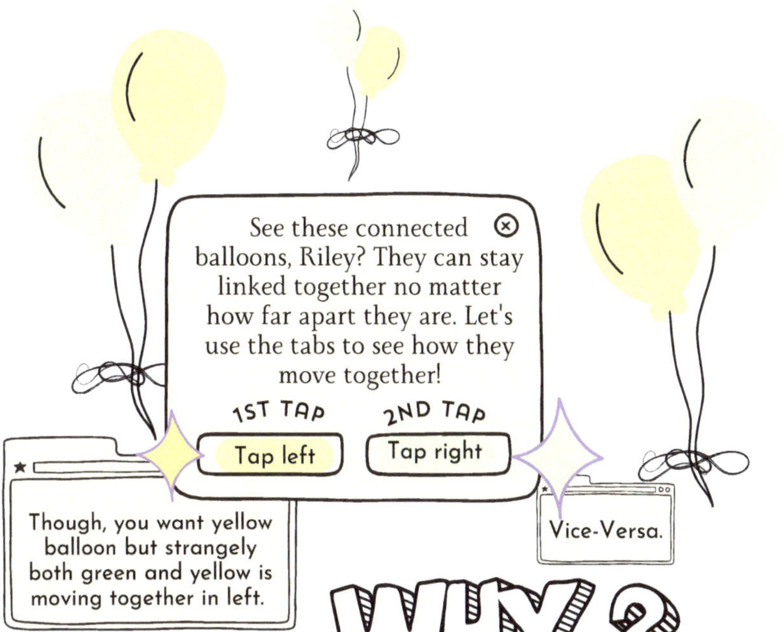

See these connected balloons, Riley? They can stay linked together no matter how far apart they are. Let's use the tabs to see how they move together!

1ST TAP: Tap left
2ND TAP: Tap right

Though, you want yellow balloon but strangely both green and yellow is moving together in left.

Vice-Versa.

WHY?

Sometimes, particles can become connected in a special way called quantum entanglement. Even if they are far apart, what happens to one particle can affect the other!

PARENT NOTE

Quantum Entanglement: When particles become connected, what happens to one can affect the other, even at a distance. It's like they have a secret way of staying linked!

Quantum computers use quantum physics to do incredibly fast calculations. They work with bits called qubits that can be both 0 and 1 at the same time!

> Riley: Look at this little champ! Quantum computers are super fast and can do amazing calculations.

Quantum Computing: Using quantum physics to create computers that can do incredibly fast calculations.

Quantum mechanics helps us understand how the smallest parts of our world work, said Riley. Let's learn more about it together, after milk.

Quantum mechanics is the branch of physics that studies how tiny particles like atoms and electrons behave. It helps scientists understand the rules of the quantum world!

One behavior of atoms is that they can spin in two directions at once until we check on them.

PARENT NOTE

Quantum Mechanics: The branch of physics that studies how tiny particles behave in the quantum world.

ELECTRON

Electrons move around an atom in different levels of energy. It's like they have different floors they can jump between! These floors decide how the atom acts.

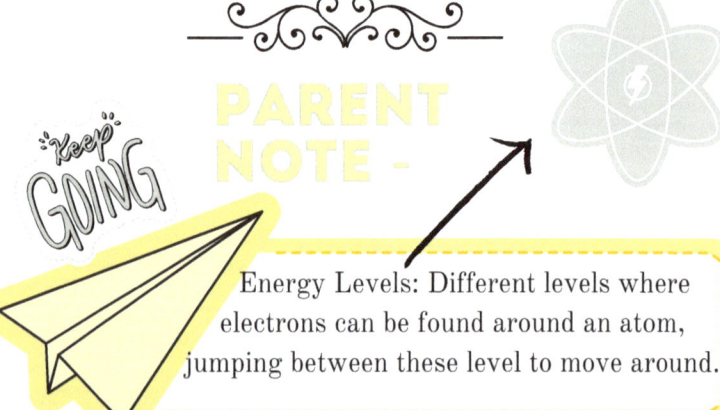

Energy Levels: Different levels where electrons can be found around an atom, jumping between these level to move around.

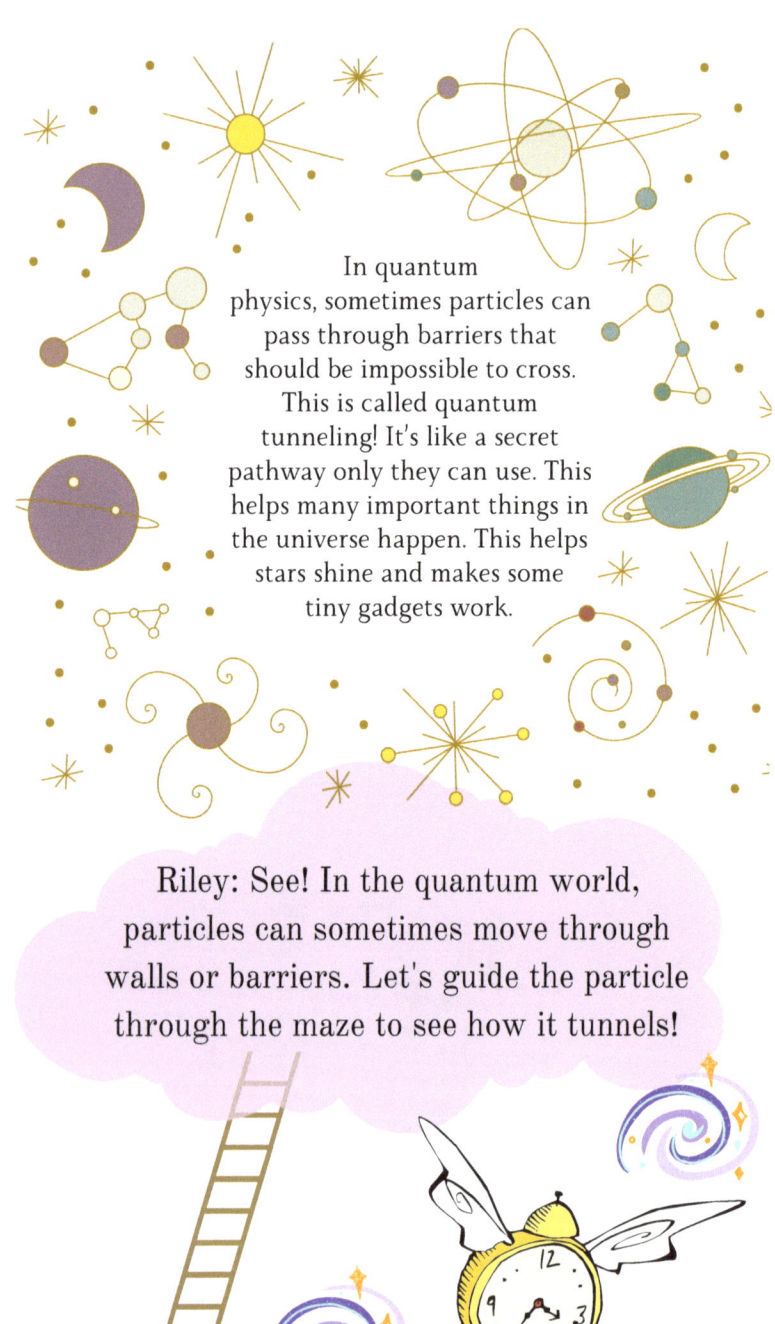

In quantum physics, sometimes particles can pass through barriers that should be impossible to cross. This is called quantum tunneling! It's like a secret pathway only they can use. This helps many important things in the universe happen. This helps stars shine and makes some tiny gadgets work.

Riley: See! In the quantum world, particles can sometimes move through walls or barriers. Let's guide the particle through the maze to see how it tunnels!

Quantum Tunneling: When particles can pass through barriers that they shouldn't be able to cross, like walking through a wall!

Have you wondered about flickering butterfly? Random motion!

Particles in the quantum world can have different states, like spinning or moving. It's like they have many different ways to show what they're doing! They can also wiggle around or even disappear and reappear in surprising ways. These states help scientists understand how tiny things work and make amazing discoveries about our world.

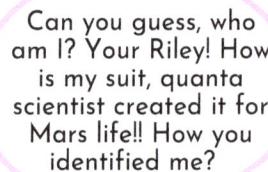

Can you guess, who am I? Your Riley! How is my suit, quanta scientist created it for Mars life!! How you identified me?

Riley: I caught you, you were able to identify me because of birth mark, right? Anyways, see these states? In the quantum world, particles can be in many different states at once. Let's spin the spinner to see how they change!

PARENT NOTE – Quantum States: Different ways particles can be in the quantum world, like spinning or moving.

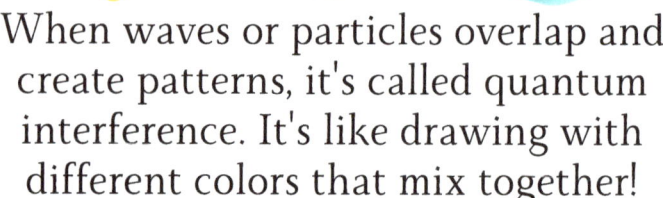

When waves or particles overlap and create patterns, it's called quantum interference. It's like drawing with different colors that mix together!

Riley: See these patterns? In the quantum world, waves and particles can overlap to create cool designs. Let's overlap them to see what happens!

PARENT NOTE -

Quantum Interference: When waves or particles overlap and create patterns in the quantum world.

You can't see ring of saturn from earth. But, we know that after using advance tools!

In quantum physics, every particle is surrounded by a quantum field. It's like having an invisible energy field around you!

Riley: Look at these fields! In the quantum world, particles have invisible energy fields around them.

PARENT NOTE -

Quantum Field: An invisible energy field that surrounds every particle in the quantum world.

Warmth of your mum's huggy is an incredible unseen energy but one in universe type! Look at this baby Koala! Aww!

Tiny, random changes in the quantum world are called quantum fluctuations. It's like bubbles popping up and disappearing!

Riley: See these changes? In the quantum world, things can randomly change all the time. Let's pop the bubbles to see how they fluctuate!

PARENT NOTE -

Quantum Fluctuations: Tiny, random changes that happen in the quantum world, like bubbles popping up and disappearing.

When particles lose their special quantum properties and start acting more like regular objects, it's called quantum decoherence.

Lets say you got a teddy bear that lits bright colorfully but once battery is over its showing you somewhat quantum decoherence. Understood!

Riley: Look! Sometimes particles lose their special quantum powers and become more normal. Look at me , left to right, when I lose all my power to cheer or create!

Quantum Decoherence: When particles lose their special quantum properties and start behaving more like regular objects.

PARENT NOTE -

Quantum entropy tells us how mixed up or uncertain a quantum system is. It's a way to measure the amount of confusion or randomness in the system. The higher the entropy, the more unpredictable the system is.

Riley: See this disorder? Quantum entropy tells us how messy things are in the quantum world. Let's arrange the particles to see their disorder!

PARENT NOTE -

Quantum Entropy: Measures how much disorder or chaos there is in a quantum system, like a messy room.

NOTE TO PARENT/GUARDIAN:

See, its not simple to familiarize a baby with Quantum Physics, but if this book is already in your hand then I believe you got great intention for your little one and not so normal parenting aspirations. So, I just want to suggest you to keep on exposing your kid to examples given here or your own and try to revive wherever you see again and again. Because of an old golden saying, kids don't learn by listening rather through observing! Daily enjoying a cookie infront of your growing baby, one day your toddler will be swinging it in air, barely even have any teeth to chew! Exposing a baby to quantum physics content can stimulate early cognitive development and curiosity. Don't stop here, keep up the extraordinary parenting drive!

BY SADAF SHAHAB AZMI, FOUNDER [UNIQVISE]

from the bottom of my heart, Thank you!

UNIQVISE

is my initiative to spread authentic and simplified informations in an unique and to the point talks. I am an university student and looking forward to change myself and elevate the condition of current chaotic world with the help of the Creator, the one! Catch me at instagram account: "UNIQVISE".

FOR BUSINESS ENQUIRIES EMAIL AT: "UNIQVISE@GMAIL.COM"

CUT OUT THIS CERTIFICATE AND DECOR YOUR CHAMP ROOM!

MINI DIPLOMA IN QUANTUM PHYSICS

This certifies that

_____

has ventured into the fascinating world of quantum physics! For your quantum leaps and bounds in early learning!

FOR CURIOUS MINDS THAT REACH FOR THE STARS AND ASK 'WHAT IF?'

DATE OF ISSUANCE:
_____

WRITE ABOVE BABY'S NAME & DAY YOU REACHED HERE!

CUT OUT THIS CERTIFICATE AND DECOR YOUR CHAMP ROOM!

www.ingramcontent.com/pod-product-compliance
Lightning Source LLC
Chambersburg PA
CBHW041506010526
44118CB00001B/34